Patterns in Nature

Program Authors

Connie Juel, Ph.D.

Jeanne R. Paratore, Ed.D.

Deborah Simmons, Ph.D.

Sharon Vaughn, Ph.D.

D1279430

Glenview, Illinois
Boston, Massachusetts
Chandler, Arizona
Upper Saddle River, New Jersey

ISBN-13: 978
ISBN-10:

6 7 8 9 10 V

CC1

Patterns in Nature

Nature's Designs

What can we learn from patterns in nature?

ANIMAL JOURNEYS

Why do animals migrate?

Our Spinning Planet

57

How do day and night affect people and animals?

STORMS 83

What can you learn about weather?

Going Green 109

How can we protect nature?

Contents

Nature's Designs

Words 2 the Wise

Go outside and look around. What do you see? Interesting shapes and colors are everywhere in nature. Read to find out about **nature's designs.**

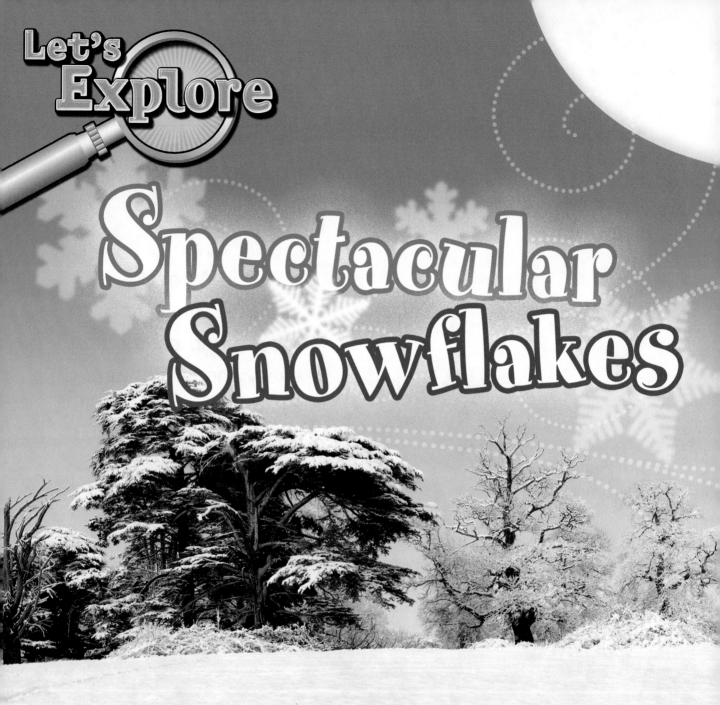

Spectacular Snowflakes

Nature is full of amazing patterns. One example is the tiny snowflake. You may have heard that no two snowflakes are alike. Is this claim really true? Let's find out.

How Snowflakes Form

A snowflake begins high in a cloud. Ice forms around a tiny speck of dust. As water freezes, it forms a six-sided pattern. From that six-sided arrangement, six icy arms grow.

A snowflake forms high up in clouds. Ice forms around a tiny speck of dust, making a six-sided pattern.

Icy arms grow out from the six-sided shape. As the snowflake moves, more arms grow.

Up in that cloud, snowflakes start to tumble around. They fall through warmer air, then colder air, then warmer air. The snowflakes' arms grow. Moving from warm to cold air causes one snowflake to have skinny arms. Another might have wider arms.

The snowflakes take different paths down to Earth. Each path is different, so each snowflake is different. A snowflake's design never repeats!

Some snowflakes are simpler than others. This one has a six-sided pattern but no arms.

This flat snowflake is shaped like a flower.

Discovering Snowflakes

Snowflakes reveal their secrets under a microscope. A microscope makes tiny things look very large. A special camera on a microscope can take pictures. Then the amazing patterns become available for us to see.

How many different types of snowflakes are there? Some say there are seven types. Others believe there are many different kinds! In any case, there is no such thing as a plain snowflake. The pictures on these pages show some different types of snowflakes.

This is a common tree-like type of snowflake. You may have seen this one on winter decorations.

The pattern of this large, fern-like type of snowflake is visible even without a microscope!

One type of snowflake is flat like a plate. Another type looks like a tree. This large snowflake can form many branches on each arm. Yet another type of snowflake looks like a leafy fern. This fern-like snowflake is so big that you can see the pattern easily without a microscope. A snowfall of these flakes can quickly cover the landscape.

Sometimes snowflakes clump together. When this happens, they lose their spectacular shapes. But they can still make a great snowman!

PATTERNS EVERYWHERE

by Fran Robbins

You're walking on a beach. Something in the waves catches your eye. You bend over to look at it. It's a starfish. It has five arms.

You're at the zoo. Two proud bighorn sheep stand on a rock. The horns of the sheep are the same shape. And they both curl around in a spiral (SPY-ruhl).

You look outside after a rain. A beautiful rainbow stretches across the landscape. You see seven different colors. Then you look at a big soap bubble in the sink. The bubble's surface displays the same colors. They are in the same order.

What are you seeing? You are seeing patterns in nature. A pattern is an arrangement that repeats itself. Many patterns of five occur in nature. So do spirals. There are color patterns in nature too. How can you learn more about these patterns in nature? Just turn the page!

starfish

sand dollar

HIGH FIVES!

Look around. Patterns of five are everywhere in nature. The starfish is one example. There are about 2,000 kinds of starfish. Most have five arms. Some have five sides but no arms. Then there's the sand dollar. This sea animal has a pattern of five on its shell.

Look at the apple on this page. It has been cut in half. Do you see the five seeds? How are they arranged?

apple

strawberry
blossom

bluebell

pear blossom

Many plants have flower petals arranged in patterns. On this page are bluebell, strawberry, and pear flowers. How many petals does each flower have?

Have you ever eaten okra (OH-kruh)? What do you see when you slice it open? Is it a pattern?

okra

15

SUPER SPIRALS

Another pattern in nature is the spiral. Can you see spirals in the seeds of the sunflower? The leaves of some ferns also have a spiral pattern as they grow. The shape of some seashells is a spiral. So are a bighorn sheep's horns. How would you like to have those huge spirals on your head?

This sunflower's seeds show a spiral pattern.

An adult bighorn sheep has large spiral horns.

This nautilus shell is the home of an ocean creature. It has a beautiful spiral shape.

The leaf of this fern has a spiral pattern.

Some spirals in nature are very large. Satellite photos of hurricanes reveal spiral shapes. The satellite photograph at right shows Hurricane Ivan. It hit the Gulf of Mexico in 2004. Another huge spiral pattern can be seen in some galaxies, including our own. Powerful telescopes make photos of these amazing spirals available so all can see them.

Why do spirals appear so often in nature? Some scientists believe that a spiral arrangement uses the least amount of energy. That makes it a smart choice for nature!

The spiral in Hurricane Ivan can be seen from above by satellite.

This galaxy is called the Pinwheel Galaxy. Can you see why?

NATURE'S DESIGNS

RED ORANGE YELLOW GREEN BLUE INDIGO PURPLE

A COLORFUL PATTERN

One of the most beautiful patterns in nature is a rainbow. Rainbows form when light shines through tiny drops of water.

The largest rainbows appear when sunlight shines through the last drops of a rain shower. Light bounces off the raindrops. The raindrops break the light into different colors. The colors of the rainbow are always in the same order. This order is red, orange, yellow, green, blue, indigo (a mix of blue and purple), and purple.

You can see this color pattern in other places too. A prism is a three-sided piece of clear glass or plastic. It breaks up light into the different colors. So does the surface of a soap bubble. You can also see a rainbow if you look through a lawn sprinkler on a sunny day.

Patterns in nature are everywhere. Just look around!

This prism separates light into different colors.

WHAT DO YOU THINK?

Do you see a rainbow before or after it rains? How does a rainbow form?

THE TALKING POT

by Bonnie Martinez • illustrated by Carlos Caban

Justin Sandoval gazed at his grandmother's clay pots. Some were lined up on shelves in his mother's kitchen. They were beautiful. All the pots were rounded. Each had a small opening at its top.

But the best thing about the pots was their color. They were all black. Some of the black parts were so shiny that Justin could see himself. Other parts were dull, like ash.

In the distance, Justin could see the great rock called Black Mesa (MAY-suh). It was red, orange, and yellow. When a snowfall covered its flat top, it looked white. The rock looked black only when the sky was dark or when it rained.

Justin loved to look at Black Mesa. He loved the way it stood out against the sky. A long time ago, his people had lived on top of the huge rock. Now the Pueblo (PWEB-loh) people made their home in the village.

Justin set out for his grandmother's workshop. He couldn't wait to see the pot she was making today. It was a special one. Soon he would paint his own pattern on it.

Justin walked past the adobe* (uh-DOH-bee) homes of his neighbors. He liked living in an adobe house. It made him feel that he was part of nature.

*adobe a mix of clay, sand, and mud

Soon Justin reached his grandmother's workshop. Bins of clay were scattered around the shop. Justin sometimes helped his grandmother dig up the clay. It was available in their village.

Justin stood quietly by his grandmother. There were many steps in the process of making a pot. First, she rolled out long snakes of clay. Then she layered the snakes on top of each other. Carefully, she built up the sides of the pot. Finally, she left a small hole at the top.

"Is it almost done?" Justin asked.

"Almost," she replied. "We must take it outside to dry."

Later, when the pot was almost dry, Justin helped his grandmother scrape the sides smooth.

"What design should I choose?" Justin wondered.

"You must choose a design that speaks to you," Justin's grandmother told him.

"Do your designs speak to you?" Justin asked.

"Yes, they do," his grandmother replied. She paused in her work and picked up a finished pot. The pot had a pattern of clouds around it.

"This design reminds me that rain is important to us," she explained. "Rain helps our crops grow and gives us life."

Justin nodded. He knew that his people's pots had patterns based on nature. Some people liked a feather design that repeated. Others chose arrangements of birds, fish, snakes, or waves.

"I want my design to say something special," Justin told his grandmother. "It should tell people about our landscape or how we live. It should talk about the Pueblo people."

His grandmother smiled. "You can paint your pot tomorrow morning," she said. "Then we will bake it."

Justin felt uneasy about his choice. "I want my first design to be a good one," he told himself. "But I want it to be different from other designs."

That evening, Justin took his favorite walk around the village. He came to the edge of the desert. He looked up. Rising up in front of him, as always, was Black Mesa.

"That's it!" Justin cried.

Early the next morning, Justin went to his grandmother's workshop. He told her his idea.

"That's perfect!" she said.

His grandmother prepared the oven. Justin painted his design on the pot. Finally, the pot went into the oven.

After the oven cooled, Justin's grandmother carefully removed the pot. Justin held it up as his grandmother admired it.

"Your pot looks just like Black Mesa," she said. "It tells our story. It shows where we live."

Justin looked across the desert at Black Mesa and smiled.

What Do You Think?

What does Justin's grandmother do first to make a pot?

I Wish I Knew

by Beverly McLoughland

Winter,
I wish I knew
The way you make
Each snowflake new,
Just how you think up
Each design—

Winter,
I wish I knew
The secret of your mind.

Sunflakes

by Frank Asch

If sunlight fell like snowflakes,
gleaming yellow and so bright,
we could build a sunman,
we could have a sunball fight,
we could watch the sunflakes
drifting in the sky.
We could go sleighing
in the middle of July
through sundrifts and sunbanks,
we could ride a sunmobile,
and we could touch sunflakes—
I wonder how they'd feel.

Word Play

Each phrase tells the meaning of a vocabulary word. Can you guess what the words are?

1. snow covering the ground
2. to do something over and over
3. to make something known
4. the land you see around you

Making Connections

Suppose Justin were to paint another pot. Which of the patterns in nature that you read about might he choose to paint on his pot? Tell why you think so.

On Paper

What is your favorite pattern in nature? Why do you like it? Write about it.

Answers for Word Play: snowfall, repeat, reveal, landscape

Contents

ANIMAL JOURNEYS

Let's Explore

Words 2 the Wise

Animal journeys are often from a winter home to a summer home. As you read, think about the reasons animals make these journeys.

Let's Explore

ANIMALS
ON THE MOVE

Have you ever wanted to move because of the weather? Sometimes it is too hot. Sometimes it is too cold. Fortunately, we have air conditioners and heaters. But what do animals do?

Some animals travel, or migrate, to new climates. Animals migrate from one place to another usually when seasons change.

DURING THE DRY SEASON IN AFRICA, ANIMALS LIKE THESE ZEBRAS MIGRATE TO FIND FOOD.

HUMPBACK WHALES MIGRATE EACH YEAR TOWARD THE WARMER WATERS OF THE EQUATOR.

Many kinds of animals migrate. Animals may travel a few miles or thousands of miles. Some migrate every year. Others migrate just once in a lifetime. Many follow the same routes each time.

Some animals migrate to start new families. Humpback whales swim to warmer waters each winter. They give birth to baby humpback whales, called calves. Salmon migrate to lay eggs. These fish swim from the ocean into rivers.

Animals often migrate to places where food is easier
to find. Warmer climates have more food for most animals.

The trip does not always have to be long. Dall sheep
live near the tops of mountains. In the winter they move
down the mountain. Less snow falls there. The sheep can
find food more easily.

Some fish live near the water's surface in summer.
They move to deeper waters in winter to stay warm.

Migration can be dangerous. Animals may hit bad weather. They may get sick or too tired to go on. They may even lose their way.

How do animals stay on course? Some use the sun and stars to guide them. Others watch for landmarks like mountains and lakes. Scientists are still trying to discover how some animals know the way to go. But scientists know one thing for sure. Animals that migrate are amazing!

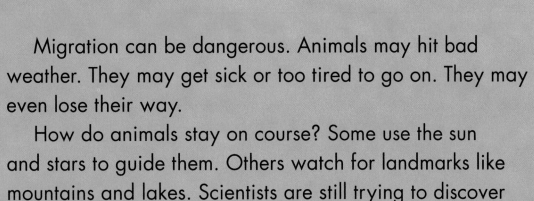

IN FALL, MONARCH BUTTERFLIES MIGRATE FROM CANADA AND THE UNITED STATES TO MEXICO. THAT'S AROUND 3,000 MILES!

FLIGHT FOR

by Danielle S. Hammelef

Would you like to visit a warm place in the winter? Many birds do. They travel thousands of miles to get there. But birds don't take these trips for fun. They migrate to survive.

Fall brings colder days in northern zones. Berries, nuts, and flowers disappear. Insects die off. Some go into hiding. Many birds depend on these foods. It gives them energy to stay warm.

SURVIVAL

Birds can fly to warmer zones when the weather gets cold. Each fall, many birds make a long trip south.

Birds are made for long flights. They have strong wings. Their bones are hollow. This makes them very light.

Most birds that migrate eat extra food before leaving. This gives them more energy. They will need it. They fly many hours each day. Some birds don't even take time to eat during the trip.

Birds' feathers are strong and flexible.

39

HOW DO BIRDS KNOW WHERE TO GO?

Birds don't carry maps. They don't use compasses. And they can't stop and ask directions. So how do they return to the same places each year?

Birds use several tricks to find their way. Birds that fly by day use landmarks to guide them. They follow rivers, mountains, and coastlines. Some birds use the sun. They watch where the sun is as they fly.

Saw-whet owls eat "on the fly." They catch insects while flying in the air.

Geese will spend up to 12 hours a day eating. They eat roots, leaves, and grasses.

Many Canada geese and many songbirds travel at night. They rest and feed during the day. And they fly after dark. The winds are calmer and temperatures are cooler at night.

Birds that fly at night use the stars to guide them. What about cloudy nights? Birds follow the wind.

WHAT TRAVEL STYLES DO BIRDS USE?

Different birds have different flight styles. Canada geese flap their wings nonstop. That takes lots of energy.

Geese fly in a V shape when migrating.

Have you ever seen geese flying in a V shape? Geese fly in a V to save energy. They create small puffs of air like wind when they flap their wings. The geese in back get a little lift from the wind. So the geese take turns leading. Geese also fly in a V so they can see and hear each other. They are less likely to get lost.

Other birds save energy by soaring. They spread out their wings and ride the wind. Soaring birds often get a "free ride."

DO MIGRATION PATHS CHANGE?

Sometimes people affect the migration paths of animals. During the winter months many trumpeter swans migrated from Canada to the United States. But in the early 1900s, these swans were hunted as a source of food and for their feathers. Because of this they nearly became extinct. Something needed to be done.

The trumpeter swan is the largest native swan in North America.

Different groups of people helped create refuges for these swans. People in these refuges helped care for and feed the swans. Over time the population slowly grew. But soon the swans got used to the free food and many no longer migrated to Canada during the warmer months. Because of this, some refuges decided to stop feeding the swans.

Trumpeter swans can fly up to 80 miles per hour!

These young birds will soon learn to fly and migrate with the others.

As the days get longer, birds fly back north. They are ready to enjoy the food that waits for them there.

Millions of birds migrate every fall and spring. Watch for birds on the move during these seasons. You may not know where they're headed, but they do!

WHAT DO YOU THINK?

What tools do birds use when they migrate?

WILDLIFE WELCOME!

BY ELIZA REDDING
ILLUSTRATED BY LINDA HOLT AYRISS

How "wild" is the space around your home? Do you hear squirrels chattering outside your window? Are bees buzzing? Do birds and butterflies fill the air?

Do you wish more wildlife visited your yard? You can make the land around your home a better place for animals. Just remember three key things: water, shelter, and food. Animals need all three to survive. These simple steps can attract more wild animals to your backyard.

KEY 1 WATER

Wild animals drink water from puddles, streams, or lakes. They also use water to keep clean. Yes, even wild animals take baths! Some animals lay eggs in water too. Sometimes water is hard to find. It may dry up in summer. It may freeze in winter.

How can you help? Set up a birdbath to give animals water all year. You can buy one, or you can make your own. An upside down garbage can lid or pie pan works well.

STEP 1 BUILD BIRDBATH

HOMEMADE BATH

STORE-BOUGHT BATH

Watch carefully for smaller visitors that stop for a drink.

Birds don't like deep water. Fill your birdbath with about three inches of water. Then add a few rocks to give the birds something to stand on. Rocks also keep the birdbath from turning over.

Put your birdbath where you can observe animal visitors. Birds probably won't be the only visitors. Squirrels, chipmunks, and insects may visit too. In the winter you can use a heater to keep water from freezing.

STEP 2 PREPARE FOR VISITORS

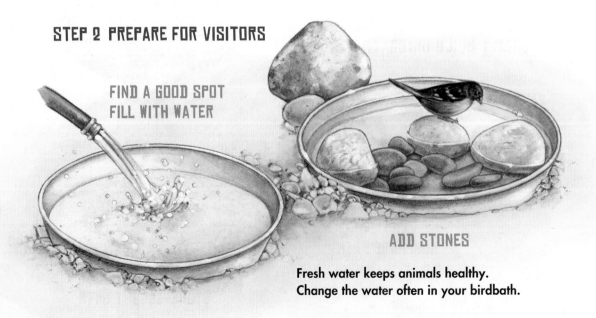

FIND A GOOD SPOT
FILL WITH WATER

ADD STONES

Fresh water keeps animals healthy.
Change the water often in your birdbath.

KEY 2 SHELTER

Animals need shelter. Shelter might be a patch of tall grass or a large woodpile. Here are shelters you can make.

BUILD A TOAD HOUSE

Toads are helpful. They eat insects. Build them a house! You need a clay flower pot and a small shovel.

Find a shady spot in your yard. Dig a hole big enough for half of the pot to fit in.

Put some soil and dead leaves inside the pot. After a few days, observe the house. Have the leaves and soil moved? If so, a toad has moved in!

SUPPLIES

TOAD HOUSE IN DIRT

During the day, toads need a cool, damp place to hide.

GO BATTY

Are mosquitoes bugging you? Invite bats to your yard. They eat their weight in insects every night.

Add a bat house to your backyard. Put up your bat house in late winter. Bats will find it when they return in spring.

Nail your bat house to a tree, pole, or building. It should face south or southeast. That way it will catch the morning sun. Hang the house at least 15 feet off the ground.

BAT HOUSE

FOR THE BIRDS

One size fits all? Not when it comes to birdhouses. Birds are picky about where they nest. Some birds like houses up in trees. Some like houses attached to poles. Some like to nest on shelves. All birdhouses should be made of wood. This lets water and heat escape.

Keep birds safe and healthy. Place birdhouses where hungry animals cannot reach them. Be sure to clean out your birdhouse in the fall.

TREE HOUSE   POLE HOUSE

Hummingbirds eat nectar from flowers. They also sip sugar water from a feeder.

KEY 3 FOOD

Plants are the best food source in your yard. Butterflies and other insects will visit to feed on flowers. Squirrels and birds will snack on fruits, nuts, and berries.

About 60 million people in the U.S. feed birds. You can too! Use different feeders and foods to get the most birds.

Some birds eat suet (SOO-it), or animal fat. You can hang suet in a netted bag. Or try spreading it on pinecones. Roll the cones in seeds for an extra treat.

SEEDS AND BERRIES FOR BIRDS

PLANTS AND FLOWERS

PINE CONE FEEDER

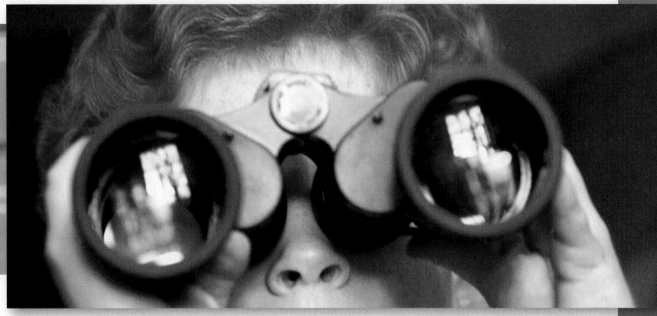

It's fun to watch wildlife in your own backyard!

START WILDLIFE WATCHING

It may take some time for wildlife to discover changes in your yard. But soon you'll see more animals out your window. Enjoy your new neighbors!

WHAT DO YOU THINK?

Why would a backyard make a good home for wildlife?

Where Birds Vacation

What types of birdhouses have you seen? Birdhouses come in all shapes and sizes. Many artists, architects, and builders like to design birdhouses.

A group of students in Australia built and painted homes for people. Then they planned a new project. They made homes for birds! The students used the same skills that they used when building houses for people. They just made the houses smaller.

Painting "The Resort" birdhouse.

Doug Harnes built an entire "birdhouse city"! His first birdhouse in the "city" was a small model of an old hotel. It is four feet tall and has 80 rooms. Doug's birdhouse city was on its way!

The whole community got involved in building Birdhouse City. Schools, businesses, and individuals of all ages helped to build over 90 birdhouses. Many of the birdhouses are copies of old buildings in the area.

4 You 2 Do

Word Play

Find words used in the selections and this week's vocabulary words to complete the acrostic puzzle.

M
I
G
R
A
Toad
E

Making Connections

What can you and your classmates do to help wild animals in your neighborhood or schoolyard?

On Paper

Which animal shelter would you choose to make? Explain why.

Possible answers for Word Play: move, insects, geese, refuges, animals, toad, eat

Our Spinning Planet

Contents

Our Spinning Planet

Let's Explore

Words 2 the Wise

The sun rises and sets every day on **our spinning planet.** As you read, think about how the Earth and the sun work together to create day and night.

NIGHT AND DAY

What star is nearest to Earth? The sun! It shines its bright light on Earth. But it can't shine on the whole Earth at the same time. Only half of our planet is in the sun at one time. Let's take a look at an example.

In Japan, on December 13, it is 10:15 A.M. It is a sunny day and Kenji is in school.

This half of Earth faces the sun and receives light.

At the same moment, this half is facing away from the sun.

At this same moment, it is 7:15 P.M. at Tracey's house in Illinois. But it is still December 12, the day before. It's dark outside and soon Tracey will go to bed.

The sun seems to rise and set, but it's really Earth that moves. The Earth makes one rotation each day as it spins on its axis. The sun never moves. Kenji and Tracey don't feel the Earth spinning. But it does. It spins at a rate of over 1,000 miles per hour!

When this half of Earth rotates away from the sun, it will be night in Japan.

N

S

N

S

Earth makes a complete turn once in 24 hours.

THE AMAZING SKIES OF THE NORTH

BY KELLY ORRICO

In summer, how late does it stay light where you live? In the far Northern Hemisphere, the longest day never ends. The sun doesn't set at all!

Imagine a day when the sun won't set. In June, it only happens in the Northern Hemisphere. It happens because of the way Earth revolves around the sun.

HOW EARTH MOVES

Earth moves in two ways. It makes a circle around the sun. This is a revolution. One complete revolution is a year.

These colorful lights are called the Aurora Borealis, or Northern Lights.

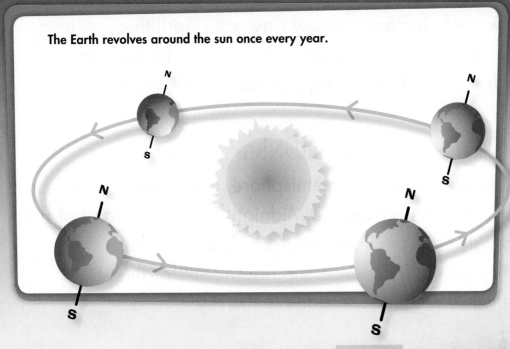

The Earth revolves around the sun once every year.

Earth also spins as it moves. This rotation causes day and night. Each full rotation is a day.

Earth is tilted. The tilt causes the seasons. During our summer, the Northern Hemisphere is pointed toward the sun. More sunlight reaches the ground during this time of year. This makes it warm.

As winter turns into spring, the days get longer. Each day the sun rises a little earlier. It sets a little later.

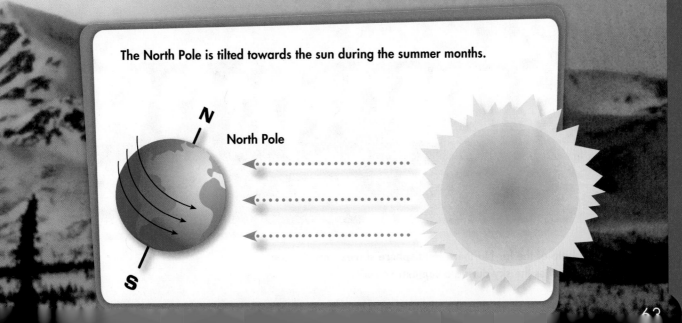

The North Pole is tilted towards the sun during the summer months.

North Pole

Daylight increases every day from April through June. By June 21, the longest day arrives. It is the summer solstice. After that the days begin to get shorter again.

WATCHING THE MIDNIGHT SUN

In the far Northern Hemisphere, the summer sun doesn't ever set! This is called the Midnight Sun. In the land of the Midnight Sun, daylight lasts for 24 hours a day.

At the North Pole, the sun doesn't set for the entire summer. It continues to shine in the sky.

This photo of the far Northern Hemisphere shows how the sun moves across the sky during a summer solstice.

SUMMER CELEBRATIONS

If you were in the North when the sun never sets, wouldn't you want to celebrate? That's just what people do in Fairbanks, Alaska.

Some people watch a baseball game. The Midnight Sun Game has been played on June 21 for more than 100 years. The game starts at 10:30 P.M., but there are no lights.

At midnight, the game stops so everyone can sing the Alaska Flag Song.

There are all kinds of games and activities during the week of the solstice. You can play soccer or baseball all night. You can dance. Stores are open all night. And one of the most unusual races anywhere starts at 10:00 P.M.

It's called the Midnight Sun Fun Run. More than 3,000 people run the race. Some wear wild costumes. People love this race.

The Midnight Sun Fun Run is the 3rd largest foot race in the state.

The North Pole is tilted away from the sun during the winter.

Now the South Pole has sunlight for 24 hours each day.

FUN IN THE ENDLESS NIGHT

Just as the sun never sets in summer, it also never rises in winter. Earth's rotation is the same, but the North Pole is tilted away from the sun. The South Pole is tilted toward the sun. The shortest day is around December 21. This is the winter solstice. What do the people of Fairbanks do during these long hours of darkness? They celebrate their nocturnal lives! They have plenty of fun activities and festivals during the winter solstice.

Alaska celebrates the winter solstice with fireworks.

A Winter Solstice Festival has plays, sleigh rides, and other fun activities.

Dog mushing races are also held during the winter. Dogs bark and jump as they pull the sleds across ice.

WONDERS IN THE WINTER SKY

One of the best ways to enjoy the Alaskan winter is also the easiest. Just go outside and look up.

During the winter solstice, you may see beautiful streams of light. They pour across the night sky like spilled paint.

Dog mushing is a popular sport in the North.

These are the Northern Lights, or the Aurora Borealis (uh-ROR-uh bor-ee-AL-is). The lights are red, green, white, orange, and yellow. Aurora is the goddess of dawn in Greek myths. Boreal comes from a word that means north.

Winter is the best time to see the Northern Lights. They are one of the most beautiful sights on Earth.

There is only one word to describe the North: *Amazing!* And the people of the North know how to enjoy it!

WHAT DO YOU THINK?

Why do you think winter is the best time to watch the Northern Lights in the North?

Plane Tired!

by Luke Heckert   illustrated by Susan Tolonen

Paris, France! I couldn't believe this vacation was real. The signs were in French. It must be true.

But I could hardly stay awake. I had jet lag. My family and I left California over sixteen hours ago. I couldn't sleep on the plane, and now I was dazed.

Time: Paris 1:00 P.M. :::::: California 4:00 A.M.

At home, it would be 4 o'clock in the morning. In Paris it was one in the afternoon. We went straight to the hotel after we landed. I flopped on the bed. Mom took her travel book out.

"Tip 16: You'll get used to a new time zone faster if you stay up," Mom read. "Let's go, Mark. We have to meet your sister at the Louvre (LOO-vruh)."

Rebecca is my big sister. She is an art student in Paris. She e-mailed us about this famous art museum.

"Hi, everyone!" Rebecca hugged us as we got out of the cab. I was so tired that I could barely lift my arms.

Rebecca was talking about a guidebook that she helped write for the museum. Mom and Dad couldn't wait to tour the Louvre. I couldn't wait to sleep!

Mom and Dad hurried inside, but Rebecca slowed down for me. "Come on!" she said. "I'll show you a suit of armor that a real knight wore."

"Did you say *night?*" I asked. I was so tired I just wanted to say good night. It was 3 P.M. here. That would be 6 A.M. at home. I blinked my eyes and shook my head.

"Rebecca, can I see that guidebook?" I asked.

The guidebook said the suit of armor was in Gallery 10.

"You must see *Mona Lisa!*" Rebecca shouted.

I didn't feel like meeting any of Rebecca's friends, so I went to check out the suit of armor.

It was really awesome. I saw one suit of armor called the *Suit of Mirrors*. I wonder if you could sleep standing up in a suit of armor. Then I saw a helmet that a gladiator had worn.

I checked the guidebook again.
A painting in Gallery 12 showed the
crowning of a king. The crown in
the painting was in Gallery 12 too.
So I went there. The picture was huge.
Sure enough, there was the same crown.

But my eyes couldn't focus anymore.
There was a bench near the painting,
so I decided to sit for a minute.

The next thing I knew, a hand was shaking my shoulder. "Did you sleep well, Mark?" a voice asked. Asleep? I looked at my watch. It was almost 5 P.M. I had been asleep for an hour!

I saw a woman about Rebecca's age. How did she know my name? I was more dazed than ever. I rubbed my eyes and said, "You must be Mona Lisa."

"I'm Marie, your sister's friend," she laughed. "You look just like your photo in Rebecca's room."

Now I was really awake. "Where is my sister?" I asked.

"Come on," Marie said.

Marie led me to the main entrance. My family was talking to a museum guard.

"Let's head to the hotel, Mark," Mom sighed. "Jet lag wins! Our vacation can wait for one night of sleep."

What Do You Think? Why was Mark so tired when he got to Paris? How was the time different?

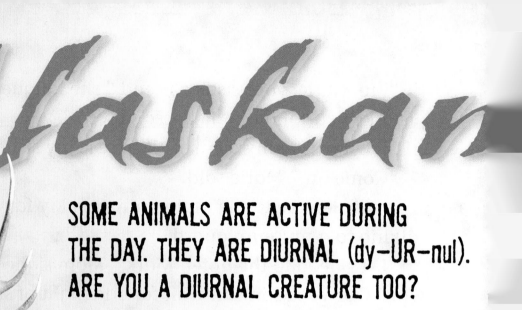

Alaskan

SOME ANIMALS ARE ACTIVE DURING THE DAY. THEY ARE DIURNAL (dy—UR—nul). ARE YOU A DIURNAL CREATURE TOO?

CARIBOU

Another name for caribou is reindeer. They have large hooves. The hooves spread out wide in the snow. They work the way snowshoes do for humans. Both caribou males and females grow antlers. In other deer families only the males have antlers.

STELLAR SEA LION

Stellar sea lions live in cold water. They eat squid, octopus, and fish.

Animals

OTHER ANIMALS ARE MOST ACTIVE AT NIGHT. THEY ARE NOCTURNAL. DURING THE DAY THEY MAY SLEEP IN BURROWS OR DENS.

BOREAL OWL

Boreal (BOR-ee-ul) means "north." This owl hunts at night for voles, mice, and small birds. Its hearing is sharper than the bald eagle's.

PORCUPINE

These porcupines are the second largest rodents in Alaska.

DIURNAL ANIMALS DO THEIR HUNTING DURING THE DAY. THEY SLEEP AT NIGHT.

MOOSE

The moose is the largest member of the deer family. Alaskans hunt moose more than any other large animal. Bears and wolves hunt moose too.

BALD EAGLE

These great birds hunt during the day. They use their sharp eyesight to spot fish. The eagle uses both hearing and sight when it hunts.

NOCTURNAL ANIMALS HUNT AT NIGHT. THEY HAVE SPECIAL ADAPTATIONS THAT HELP THEM.

FLYING SQUIRREL

Another name for the flying squirrel is night glider. It glides from tree to tree.

LYNX

The lynx is a night hunter on the tundra. It hunts and lives alone. This cat eats mice, birds, and red squirrels. The snowshoe hare is its favorite prey.

4 you or 2 Do

Word Play

The word *nocturnal* means "night." *Solstice* has to do with the sun. Answer the questions below. Each answer has two words that rhyme. Hint: Use *night* or *sunny*.

What is an airplane ride in the dark? _____

What are bright coins? _____

What is the moon at 10 P.M.? _____

What is a yellow rabbit? _____

Making Connections

During the summer solstice in Alaska, people must sleep while the sun shines. When people travel across the ocean, they must get used to a different time zone. How are these two experiences alike?

On Paper

Most people have jobs during the day. Describe and tell about a nighttime job.

Contents

STORMS

Words 2 the Wise

Sometimes **storms** are predictable, and other times they are not. What do you know about weather? As you read, think about how the weather changes where you live.

Let's Explore

WEIRD

If it's raining cats and dogs, it's raining hard. But have you ever heard of raining frogs?

A shower of frogs is a weather phenomenon (fuh-NOM-uh-non). It can be explained. But it is strange. First, a wind storm or tornado passes over a pond filled with frogs. The strong wind picks up some frogs. Later, the wind dies down. The frogs fall back to Earth. It seems to be raining frogs!

It never *really* rains cats and dogs, but it has rained frogs and fish.

WEATHER

Another weather
phenomenon is the sun halo.
Ice crystals in a cloud cause this halo,
or ring, of light around the sun. The sunlight
reflects against the ice crystals making a perfect
circle. Sometimes this means it is going to rain
or snow. Have you ever seen a halo around the
moon? This is also caused by ice crystals.
Have you experienced a weather
phenomenon in your area? Watch for signs
of weird weather near you. Nature can
surprise us with some incredible sights.

HOW DID THE ANIMALS KNOW?

by Jesse Green

Giant waves destroyed many towns on the coasts of Asia and Africa on December 26, 2004. This weather disaster was called a tsunami (soo-NAH-mee). Tsunami is a Japanese word that means "harbor wave." An earthquake off the coast of Indonesia (In-doh-NEE-zhuh) caused this tsunami.

The tsunami that hit in 2004 was shocking. Thousands of people lost their lives. Many places were swallowed up by the ocean waves.

The communities hit hardest by the tsunami did not know about the coming disaster. They did not have a warning system. Nature gave signals. But many people didn't know how to read them.

One of these signals was the behavior of the animals. They could sense the danger.

This village in Indonesia was destroyed by the tsunami in 2004.

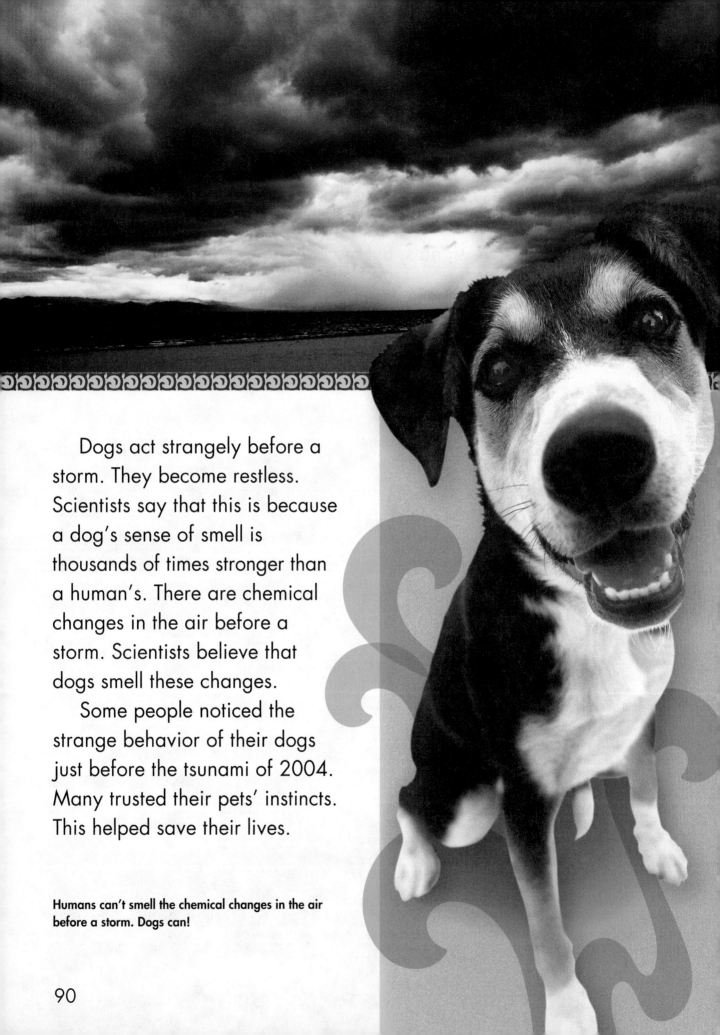

Dogs act strangely before a storm. They become restless. Scientists say that this is because a dog's sense of smell is thousands of times stronger than a human's. There are chemical changes in the air before a storm. Scientists believe that dogs smell these changes.

Some people noticed the strange behavior of their dogs just before the tsunami of 2004. Many trusted their pets' instincts. This helped save their lives.

Humans can't smell the chemical changes in the air before a storm. Dogs can!

90

One young girl in India thought she would be safe in her concrete house. The house was only forty feet from the shore. A huge wave was about to crush it. The family dog sensed that there was danger. It barked. And it kept nudging the girl to go away. The girl followed her dog. They went up a hill before the wave hit. They were safe.

Dogs are not the only animals that sensed the tsunami.

Birds and fish seemed to sense the danger of the tsunami too. Many flamingos left coastal areas before the tsunami hit. They flew to a higher place. There they were able to survive.

Animals also picked up on signals from other animals. Birds in the air noticed how schools of fish were swimming. So the birds flew in a different direction. Animals on the land saw the birds' behavior. This caused them to leave the areas along the coast.

Before the tsunami, flamingos left the area where they lay eggs.

Wildlife communicated danger to one another. Humans observed the animals' behavior and escaped.

Zoo animals also behaved strangely before the tsunami hit. Some animals tried to break free. Others backed into the corners of their cages. And monkeys refused to eat bananas. The sense of danger took away their appetites.

In Thailand, tourists heard the loud trumpeting of elephants. The elephants were afraid. Some actually broke free from their chains. At first people were confused. Then people took the elephants' behavior as a signal. They ran away too.

93

A change in the way birds fly signals danger might be near.

What gave animals warning of the 2004 tsunami? Why didn't many people know what was coming? Animals have stronger senses than people. They can pick up on sounds, smells, temperature changes, and vibrations of the earth. They also notice the behavior of other animals around them. This gives them clues to possible danger.

These instincts help animals survive.

94

Could a tsunami like the one that hit in 2004 strike the United States? Yes. But now, we have two different warning systems. We have weather reports that can alert people in time. And we can read the signals that nature and its animals give us.

Watch your dog, cat, or bird the next time a storm is approaching. Is your pet behaving strangely?

WHAT DO YOU THINK?

How are the animals' reactions to the tsunami the same? How are they different?

TAITO
AND THE GULLS

BY JULIE LAVENDER ILLUSTRATED BY MELANIE HALL

I could watch gulls all day.

I run along the edge of the water, trying to stay with the gulls. The leader is unpredictable. It takes a dive. Then it flies the other way. The rest of the gulls follow. One by one, they splash into the water. They bounce and bob with the waves.

I sit down and dig my toes into the sand. The gulls dip their bills into the water, grabbing fish to eat.

"Fish! Oh, no!"

"Taito!" (TAY-toh)

It's my mother. I was supposed
to be catching fish for the feast tonight!

"Taito, you've been gone a long time." She
looks unhappy. "Where are the fish?"

I hang my head because I'm in trouble.
"Mother, I haven't caught any fish. I was
watching the gulls and forgot what I should
have been doing. I'm sorry."

"Taito, your father told you to catch fish
for tonight's big feast. Come home now."

I'm nervous when I see my father and my great-grandfather. "Your net is empty," my father says. "This is not the first time you didn't listen. This has to stop. You must learn."

Father thinks for a moment. He says, "Since you didn't help prepare for the feast, you may not attend."

98

I don't argue. I didn't do my job. Now I'll miss the feast. There is disappointment in Great-grandfather's eyes. He has often told me I should listen to instructions as closely as I listen to his stories.

Great-grandfather is very wise. He teaches me about our people, the Arawak (AH-rah-wahk), and our island. He tells me stories about the sea and the animals. "The animals are your best teachers," he says. "Learn from them. Observe their ways."

Sights, sounds, and smells of the feast come to me. Music, singing, and laughter fill the air. People are dancing. I smell fish grilling. I go for a walk along the beach.

When I reach the bay, the gulls are floating on the water. The afternoon sky looks very dark. This is strange.

Suddenly, the gulls fly away from the water toward the center of the island. They disappear into the trees.

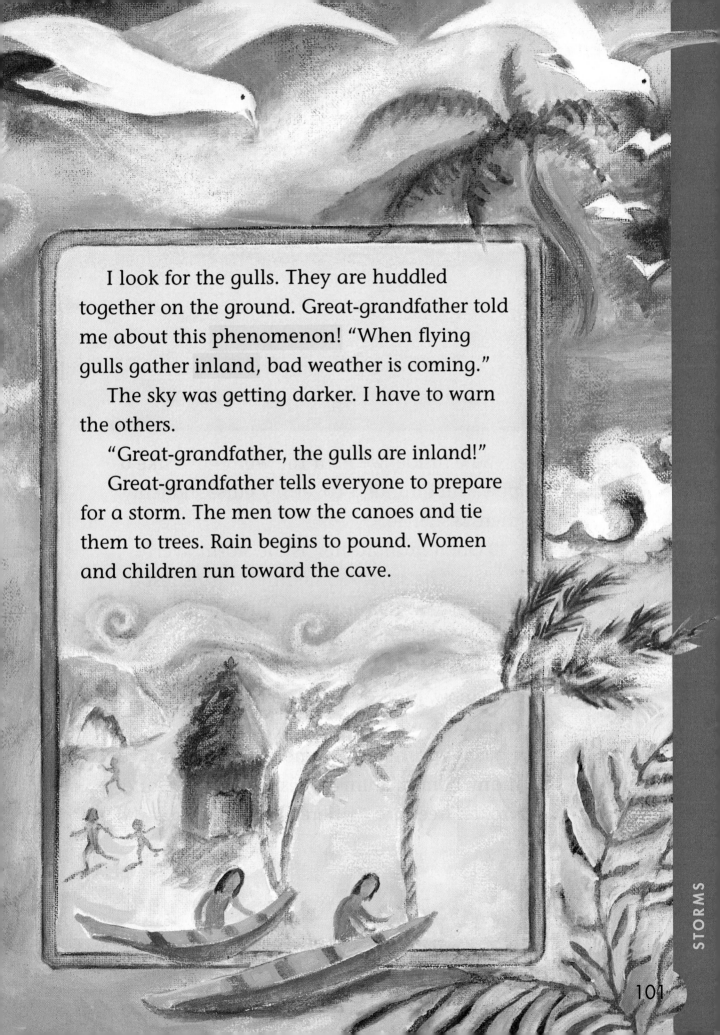

I look for the gulls. They are huddled together on the ground. Great-grandfather told me about this phenomenon! "When flying gulls gather inland, bad weather is coming."

The sky was getting darker. I have to warn the others.

"Great-grandfather, the gulls are inland!"

Great-grandfather tells everyone to prepare for a storm. The men tow the canoes and tie them to trees. Rain begins to pound. Women and children run toward the cave.

Safe inside, we hear the wind howl like a powerful animal. I cover my ears. Suddenly, there is silence.

"Great-grandfather, is the storm over?"

"No," he says. "Sometimes storms rest a while. Then their fury starts again. They can be very unpredictable."

The rain returns with the screaming wind. Somehow, I fall asleep. The next morning it is calm and quiet.

This weather phenomenon has destroyed many homes. Palm leaves, hammocks, and broken trees are scattered everywhere.

"Don't worry," Great-grandfather says.
"The storm took our homes, but it didn't take
our lives. Our village will rise again."

Adults begin to move fallen trees, and
children gather palm leaves.

I find pieces of my fishing net and wonder
about the gulls. I run to a hill overlooking the
beach. I see birds bobbing on the water. The
gulls are safe and have returned home, just
like my people.

WHAT DO YOU THINK?
Compare the first time Taito watches
the gulls to the second time.

Is It Going to Rain?

Weather forecasters can predict when it is going to rain by reading a barometer. A barometer (buh-RAH-muh-ter) is an instrument that measures air pressure. On TV weather reports, you hear forecasters talking about high pressure and low pressure. They know this from reading a barometer.

When the air pressure begins falling, that is a good sign that it is going to rain. You can make your own barometer to see if it is going to rain.

How to Make a Barometer

All the materials needed to make a barometer might be in your classroom or kitchen.

Materials
- a glass
- water
- empty soda bottle
- food coloring

food coloring

water

glass

soda bottle

1 Use a glass that can hold an upside down soda bottle. It is important that the soda bottle fit tightly inside the glass without touching the bottom of the glass.

2 Take the bottle out of the glass and fill the glass with water. Add food coloring to the water. This will help you see the water level.

3 Slowly place the uncapped, empty soda bottle upside down in the glass of water. Notice the water level in the soda bottle.

4 Watch for a change in water level.

If the water level drops, the air pressure has decreased. A decrease in air pressure means rain is on its way!

4 YOU 2 DO

Word Play

Use a trick to remember how to spell *phenomenon*. Start with *p*. Then think of these other words in order.

p

a 2-letter word _____

a 2-letter word _____

a 3-letter word _____

a 2-letter word _____

Put the smaller words together in order to spell the whole word.

Making Connections

You read about weird weather this week. How did animals warn people of danger?

On Paper

Choose an animal that you read about. Make a comic strip about a storm and an animal that warns people of danger.

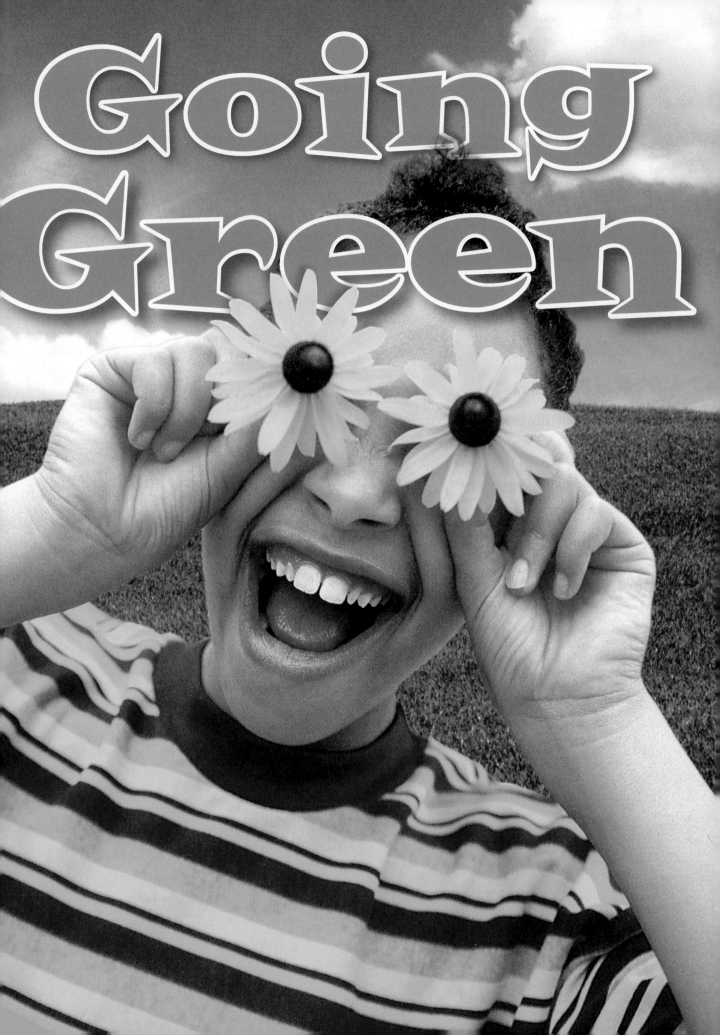

Going Green

Contents

Going Green

Let's Explore

Words 2 the Wise

We change nature when we don't take care of it. That's why people who want to protect nature are **going green.** Read to find out what you can do.

786

Let's Explore

RECYCLING

Take one last sip from your soda can. Head for the trash can. Wind up to throw it away. STOP!

That can needs a second chance. It could be melted down. It could be made into a new can. It could sit on a store shelf again!

But if you toss that can away, it will become plain old trash. Our planet does not need more trash.

AMERICANS USE 200 MILLION METAL DRINK CANS EACH DAY!

THE METAL IN CANS CAN BE MELTED EASILY. IT CAN BE USED AGAIN AND AGAIN.

DID YOU KNOW?

People tossed out one trillion drink cans between 1972 and 2003. Picture these cans lined up end to end. They could stretch to the moon and back 158 times!

People throw away 2 million cell phones each week. These phones leak dangerous chemicals. They can poison the land around them.

DID YOU KNOW?

Trash does not just go underground. It goes into the oceans too. More than 14 billion pounds of trash end up there each year. Plastic bags and balloons cause problems. They choke and kill sea turtles, fish, and seals.

Companies in the United States use enough paper to circle the planet 20 times. That is in just *one day*!

PAPER PRODUCTS MAKE UP ALMOST HALF OF ALL OUR TRASH.

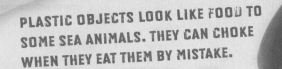
PLASTIC OBJECTS LOOK LIKE FOOD TO
SOME SEA ANIMALS. THEY CAN CHOKE
WHEN THEY EAT THEM BY MISTAKE.

DID YOU KNOW?

There is some good news about trash!

One ton is equal to 2,000 pounds. Each ton of recycled paper saves 17 trees!

We recycle about 113,000 metal cans every minute!

People who recycle help save energy. They protect the air, land, and water. They save money too.

SO NOW YOU KNOW. WHAT'S YOUR PLAN FOR YOUR SODA CAN—AND ALL YOUR OTHER TRASH?

SAFER ENERGY

The search is on!

by Jennifer Lewis

Energy is an important part of our lives. Think about it. We flip a switch and the light is on. We press a button and watch a TV show. We press a pedal and the car moves.

Most of our energy comes from coal, oil, and natural gas. These resources are found underground. They take millions of years to form. And they are nonrenewable. This means that once they are gone, we cannot make more.

Electricity in our homes powers many of the machines we use daily.

Some scientists predict that we may soon run out of these resources. They are costly. But worst of all, they pollute the air, land, and water.

There are over 6 billion people on Earth. And it keeps growing. As the population grows, so does our need for energy. We need to find new sources of energy. Today, people are looking to the sky, the sun, and even the sea for help!

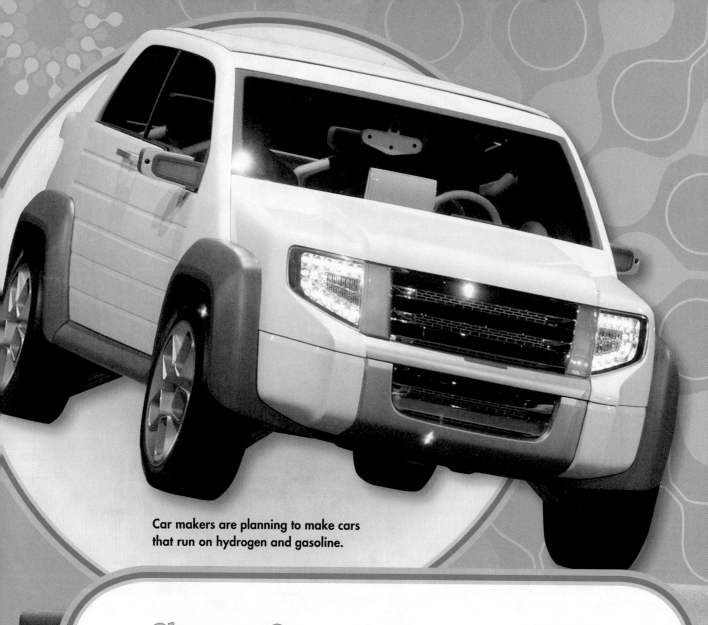

Car makers are planning to make cars that run on hydrogen and gasoline.

Cleaner Cars

There are more than 240 million cars and trucks on our roads today. Almost all of them burn gasoline for fuel. When cars burn gasoline, they cause air pollution. Many scientists believe this kind of pollution is making our planet warmer. This could be harmful over time.

A chemical called hydrogen (HI-dro-jen) may be the answer. It's cleaner than gasoline or electricity. Hydrogen cars give off only heat and water!

Hydrogen cars are not available yet. They cost too much to build and their tanks cannot store enough hydrogen. But scientists hope to work out these problems.

A Ray of Hope

Other people look to the skies to solve our energy problems. They want to use energy from the sun. This is called solar energy. Solar cells collect sunlight. They turn it into energy.

This house uses solar energy. Solar cells on the roof collect sunlight.

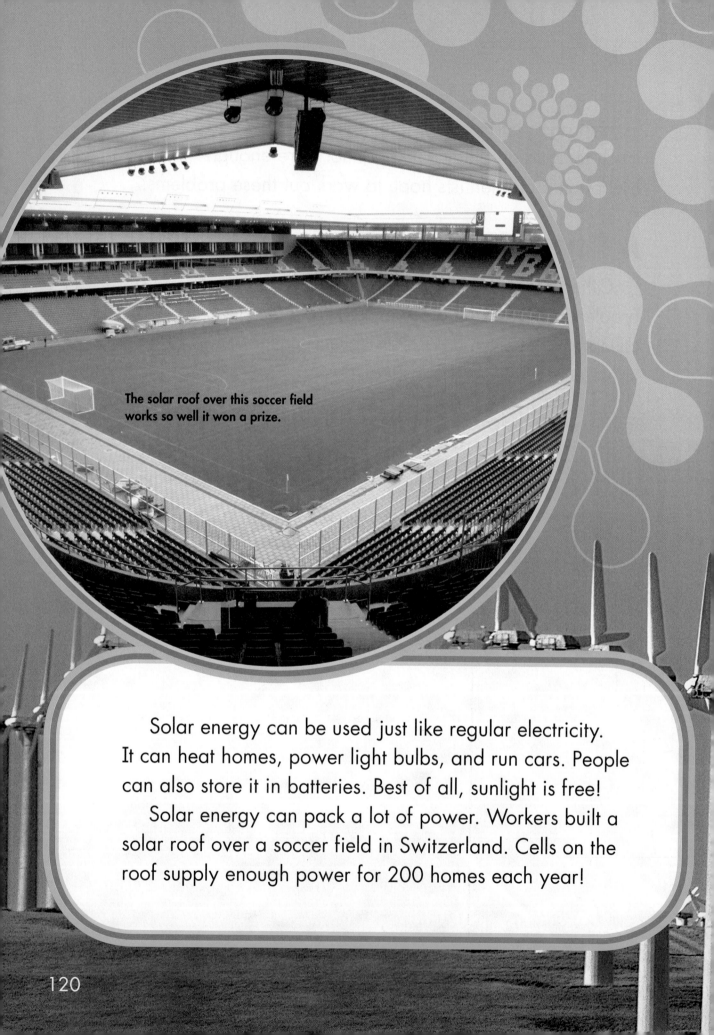

The solar roof over this soccer field works so well it won a prize.

Solar energy can be used just like regular electricity. It can heat homes, power light bulbs, and run cars. People can also store it in batteries. Best of all, sunlight is free!

Solar energy can pack a lot of power. Workers built a solar roof over a soccer field in Switzerland. Cells on the roof supply enough power for 200 homes each year!

It's a Breeze

If you fly kites or sail boats, you know all about wind power. It can be powerful.

Some places in the United States use wind power for energy. The wind spins blades on a giant tower. The spinning blades make electricity.

Wind towers work well along coasts, over hilltops and mountains, and across plains.

Some areas get energy from "wind farms." These are rows of towers with giant blades.

Go with the Flow

Dams are another great energy source. Dams make hydropower. *Hydro* means water. As water flows through the dam, it spins a turbine (TUR-byn). The turbine is like a giant barrel or wheel. It makes electricity as it spins.

Hydropower has been around for a very long time. But it wasn't always used to make electricity. Hydropower was used for grinding grain and watering crops. The great thing is that water is renewable!

Hydropower dams provide electricity to millions of people.

Ocean waves may be used for electricity one day.

Today, people are studying ways to use the oceans for hydropower. Waves from the oceans might one day warm your house!

Wind, sun, and water are renewable energy sources. They are easily collected. They are cleaner than coal and oil. This would help prevent more pollution.

Who knows? Some day you might drive a solar car. Or you might have a wind tower in your backyard!

What Do You Think?

Why do we need to find other ways to get electricity?

RACING WITH

BY STEVE HALEY

Cars line up to start the race. Some cars look like spaceships. Most are shaped like waffles with a cherry on top. These cars are ready for the North American Solar Challenge.

These cars don't use gas. They run on sunlight. Square solar cells cover most of the car. The cells collect sunlight. They change sunlight into energy that the car can use. Solar energy has benefits. It does not pollute, and it won't get used up.

UNIVERSITY OF MINNESOTA CAR

124

WATERLOO AND MINNESOTA CAR

Most solar cars today only have enough room for the driver.

FIRE IT UP!

Let's follow the North American Solar Challenge that took place in 2005. This race went from Austin, Texas, to Canada. Drivers called it a "rayce." The name combined the words *race* and *rays*.

Cars raced for eleven days. They traveled 2,500 miles. The car with the fastest time won.

Teams spent thousands of hours building their cars. Each car had to be able to reach a speed that regular cars can go on the highway.

GOING GREEN

While building and racing these cars has its benefits, solar cars aren't for everyday transportation. They don't store enough power. They can only run during the day. And they have room for only one person.

Racers have to experiment to find new ways to store energy.

AND THEY'RE OFF!

The race began at 9:00 A.M. Drivers had to follow road rules and race rules. The cars traveled at the same speed as regular traffic.

IOWA STATE CAR

Solar cars can't be on the road nonstop. They can only drive during the day. Bright, sunny days help the cars go faster and farther. The cars can store some solar energy to use when it's cloudy.

As the sun set, day one of the race ended. A car from the University of Michigan was in the lead. Still, it was too early to predict a winner.

University of Michigan crew takes the lead on the first day.

UNIVERSITY OF MICHIGAN CAR

This car from Iowa State University finished in 3rd place.

UNIVERSITY OF CALGARY CAR

The University of Calgary won an award for The Best Rookie Team in 2005.

On day two, a new car took the lead. It belonged to a team from Minnesota. Other cars had trouble. Rainfall slowed down some of them. One car had to drive through a hailstorm!

The racers had a long way to go. In 2001 and 2003, cars had traveled from Chicago to Los Angeles. That was only 2,200 miles.

Now the race went into two countries. No other solar car race in the world was as long.

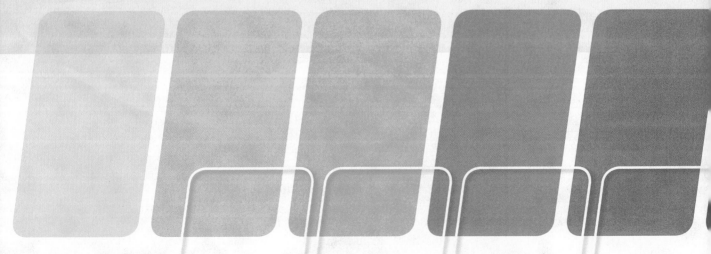

HALFWAY THERE!

Day five came. The solar cars crossed the border into Canada on that day. Midway through the race, the Minnesota team was still in the lead. They predicted they would win. But anything could happen.

The California team had high hopes for its car. They called it the Beam Machine.

On most days, the Beam Machine rolled along at 40 to 50 miles per hour.

CALIFORNIA BEAM MACHINE

WESTERN MICHIGAN SUNSEEKER

Each team hopes it has come up with the winning design.

The solar cars caused people to stare wherever they went. Each one had its own special look. One car, the Sunseeker, was bright yellow. Another car, built in Canada, had flaps like sails. The students who built it hoped the flaps would catch the wind for an extra push.

A BIG FINISH!

It was the last day of the race. Everyone wanted to know who would win. The Michigan and Minnesota teams were in a fight for the lead.

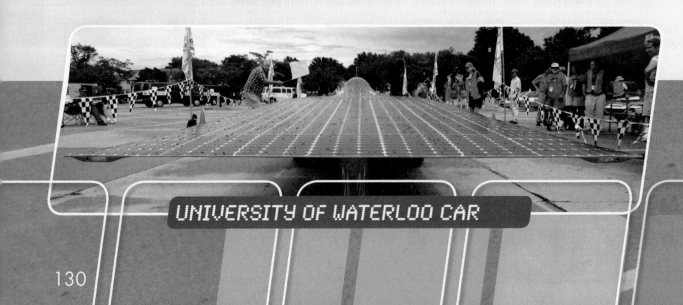

UNIVERSITY OF WATERLOO CAR

More than 10,000 people waited at the finish line. They roared with excitement when the cars came into view! The University of Michigan car finished in 53 hours, 59 minutes, and 43 seconds. It was the winner. The Minnesota team finished 11 minutes later.

The Solar Challenge takes place every two years. Teams spend years preparing. They test new designs and dream of winning!

MICHIGAN WINS THE RACE!

WHAT DO YOU THINK?

How is a solar car powered? How are solar cars different from other types of cars?

Let's Save

Creating a new bike trail. Building a playground with recycled materials. Putting up nest boxes for rare birds. What do these projects have in common? They all help protect the environment. And they all happened because kids thought of them.

Since 1971, the White House has given awards to kids who do projects like these. One of these awards is called the President's Environmental Youth Awards (PEYA). The government awards up to ten projects each year.

In 2003, scouts planted over 800 trees!

the Planet!

In 2004, local scouts won the President's Environmental Youth Award (PEYA) for their Wetland Habitat Enhancement Project. In a two-year period the scouts had planted over 1,500 trees! Even though they won in 2004, the scouts are not done yet. They plan to continue planting trees.

Every year hundreds of students show their commitment to protecting the Earth and its resources. Find out what you can do to help!

President Bush presented an award to these scouts on Earth Day.

4 You 2 Do

Word Play

Write an advertisement for a new solar car that uses one of this week's vocabulary words.

Making Connections

Which kind of energy source that you read about do you think will become common in the future? Why do you think so?

On Paper

This week you learned about how the sun, wind, and water can be used to make new energy. Choose one of these sources and explain how it protects the environment.

Glossary

ar·range·ment (ə rānj′ mənt), *NOUN.* the way or order in which things or people are arranged: *You can make a room look different by changing the arrangement of furniture.*

a·vail·a·ble (ə vā′lə bəl), *ADJECTIVE.* able to be had or gotten: *No tickets were available for the play-off game.*

be·hav·ior (bi hā′ vyər), *NOUN.* a way of acting; actions: *We rewarded the puppy's good behavior with a treat.*

ben·e·fit (ben′ ə fit), *NOUN.* anything that helps someone or something; advantage: *The vitamins in vegetables are a benefit to the health of people. PL.* **ben·e·fits.**

cell (sel), *NOUN.* a unit in a device for converting chemical or solar energy into electricity: *The new car was powered by solar cells.* PL. **cells.**

coast (kōst), *NOUN.* the land along the sea; seashore: *Many ships were wrecked on the rocky coast.*

daze (dāz), *VERB.* to make someone unable to think clearly: *She was dazed after falling from her horse.* **dazed, daz·ing.**

a in hat	ō in open	sh in she
ā in age	ȯ in all	th in thin
â in care	ô in order	₮H in then
ä in far	oi in oil	zh in measure
e in let	ou in out	ə = a in about
ē in equal	u in cup	ə = e in taken
ėr in term	u̇ in put	ə = i in pencil
i in it	ü in rule	ə = o in lemon
ī in ice	ch in child	ə = u in circus
o in hot	ng in long	

e·lec·tric·i·ty (i lek′ tris′ ə tē), NOUN. energy that can produce light, heat, or motion: *The spinning blades on wind towers produce electricity. We use electricity when we turn on a light.*

hem·i·sphere (hem′ ə sfir), NOUN. a half of the Earth's surface; Earth is divided into the Northern and Southern Hemispheres and the Eastern and Western Hemispheres: *The U.S. is in the Northern Hemisphere and in the Western Hemisphere.*

hy·dro·gen (hī′ drə jən), NOUN. a colorless gas that burns easily: *Hydrogen combines with oxygen to form water.*

in·land (in′ lənd), ADVERB. away from the coast or the border: *We traveled inland to escape the hurricane.*

land·scape (land′ skāp), *NOUN.* a view of scenery from one place: *The two hills with the valley formed a beautiful landscape.*

mi·grate (mī′ grāt), *VERB.* to go from one place to another when the seasons change: *Birds migrate south each winter.* **mi·grat·ed, mi·grat·ing.**

noc·tur·nal (nok tėr′ nl), *ADJECTIVE.* active in the night: *Owls are nocturnal creatures.*

ob·serve (əb zėrv′), *VERB.* to look at something carefully in order to learn about it; study: *I observe the stars at night.* **ob·served, ob·serv·ing.**

a	in hat	ō	in open	sh	in she
ā	in age	ȯ	in all	th	in thin
â	in care	ô	in order	TH	in then
ä	in far	oi	in oil	zh	in measure
e	in let	ou	in out	ə	= a in about
ē	in equal	u	in cup	ə	= e in taken
ėr	in term	u̇	in put	ə	= i in pencil
i	in it	ü	in rule	ə	= o in lemon
ī	in ice	ch	in child	ə	= u in circus
o	in hot	ng	in long		

pat·tern (pat′ ərn), NOUN. the way in which colors or shapes appear over and over again in order: *The wallpaper had a striped pattern.* PL. **pat·terns.**

phe·nom·e·non (fə nom′ ə non), NOUN. someone or something that is extraordinary or remarkable: *A tornado is a weather phenomenon that can cause great damage.* PL. **phe·nom·e·na.**

ref·uge (ref′ yüj), NOUN. shelter or protection from danger or trouble: *We used the old cabin in the woods as a refuge from the storm.* PL. **ref·ug·es.**

re·peat (ri pēt′), VERB. to do or make something again: *I try not to repeat my mistakes.* **re·peats, re·peat·ed, re·peat·ing.**

re·source (ri sôrs′), NOUN. something that will meet a need: *Water is a natural resource.* PL. **re·sourc·es.**

re·veal (ri vēl′), VERB. 1. to make something known: *I promised never to reveal her secret.* 2. to display or show something: *His smile revealed his white teeth.* **re·veals, re·vealed, re·veal·ing.**

rev·o·lu·tion (rev′ ə lü′ shən), NOUN. a movement in a circle or curve around some point: *It takes a year for the Earth to complete one revolution around the sun.*

ro·ta·tion (rō tā′ shən), NOUN. the act of turning around a center: *The Earth makes a complete rotation once a day.*

a in hat	ō in open	sh in she
ā in age	ȯ in all	th in thin
â in care	ô in order	ŦH in then
ä in far	oi in oil	zh in measure
e in let	ou in out	ə = a in about
ē in equal	u in cup	ə = e in taken
ėr in term	u̇ in put	ə = i in pencil
i in it	ü in rule	ə = o in lemon
ī in ice	ch in child	ə = u in circus
o in hot	ng in long	

shel·ter (shel′ tər), *NOUN.* something that covers or protects you from the weather or danger: *Trees provide shelter from the sun.*

snow·fall (snō′ fȯl′), *NOUN.* a fall of snow: *There was a snowfall late last night.*

so·lar (sō′ lər), *ADJECTIVE.* of or from the sun: *A solar panel collects sunlight.*

tsu·na·mi (sü nä′ mē), *NOUN.* a long, high sea wave caused by an underwater earthquake or submarine landslide, or other disturbance: *The tsunami hit the coast of India.*

un·pre·dict·a·ble (un′ pri dik′ tə bəl), *ADJECTIVE.* not able to be described or depended on; uncertain: *The story's ending was unpredictable.*

va·ca·tion (vā kā′ shən), *NOUN.* a time of rest or freedom from school, work, or other duties: *We spent our vacation at the beach.*

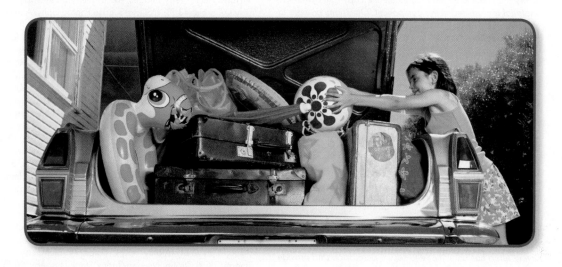

zone (zōn), *NOUN.* any of the five great divisions of the Earth's surface, bounded by imaginary lines going around the Earth parallel to the equator: *The U.S. lies in the north temperate zone.*

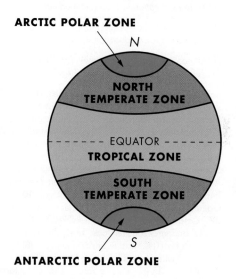

a	in hat	ō	in open	sh	in she
ā	in age	ȯ	in all	th	in thin
â	in care	ô	in order	ŦH	in then
ä	in far	oi	in oil	zh	in measure
e	in let	ou	in out	ə	= a in about
ē	in equal	u	in cup	ə	= e in taken
ėr	in term	ù	in put	ə	= i in pencil
i	in it	ü	in rule	ə	= o in lemon
ī	in ice	ch	in child	ə	= u in circus
o	in hot	ng	in long		

Acknowledgments

Text

Every effort has been made to locate the copyright owner of material reproduced in this component. Omissions brought to our attention will be corrected in subsequent editions. Grateful acknowledgment is made to the following for copyrighted material.

28 Beverly McLoughland "I Wish I Knew" by Beverly McLoughland from *Read and Understand Poetry, Grades 3–4,* Evan-Moor. Used by permission of the author.

29 Greenwillow Books, An Imprint of HarperCollins Publishers "Sunflakes" from *Country Pie* by Frank Asch. Copyright © 1979 by Frank Asch. Used by permission of HarperCollins Publishers.

Illustrations

20–26 Carlos Caban; **28** Elena Selivanova; **47–53** Linda Holt Ayriss; **70–76** Susan Tolonen; **96–102** Melanie Hall.

Photographs

Every effort has been made to secure permission and provide appropriate credit for photographic material. The publisher deeply regrets any omission and pledges to correct errors called to its attention in subsequent editions.

Unless otherwise acknowledged, all photographs are the property of Pearson Education, Inc.

Photo locators denoted as follows: Top (T), Center (C), Bottom (B), Left (L), Right (R), Background (Bkgd)

Cover: (CR) ©Tim Gainey/Alamy Images, (TL, BC) Getty Images, (CR) ©John Warden/Index Stock Imagery, (BR) Stefano Paltera/©American Solar Challenge, (CL) Stockdisc; **1** (CL) Stockdisc; **2** (T) ©Qing Ding/Shutterstock, (B) ©Royalty-Free/Corbis; **5** (C) ©R Panier/PhotoLibrary Group, Inc.; **6** (C) ©Joao Virissimo/Shutterstock, (TR) ©Khoo Si Lin/Shutterstock; **7** (CR) ©GSFC/NASA, (B) ©PMichael Photoz/AKA/PhotoLibrary Group, Inc., (B) ©Tom Merton/Getty Images; **8** (C) ©Tim Gainey/Alamy Images; **10** (C) ©Tim Gainey/Alamy Images; **12** (CR) ©Elena Elisseeva/Shutterstock, (BC) ©moodboard/Corbis; **13** (C) ©PHOTOCREO Michal Bednarek/Shutterstock; **14** (T) ©Joao Virissimo/Shutterstock, (T) ©Khoo Si Lin/Shutterstock, (B) ©Nathan Shahan/Shutterstock, (T) ©Noah Strycker/Shutterstock, (B) Photolibrary; **15** (B) ©Analia Valeria Urani/Shutterstock, (T) ©Jorgen Larsson/PhotoLibrary Group, Inc., (B) ©Lynda Schemansky/PhotoLibrary Group, Inc., (CR) ©Qing Ding/Shutterstock, (T) ©Sergey Chushkin/Shutterstock; **16** (BC) ©Geanina Bechea/Shutterstock, (BL) ©Mayskyphoto/Shutterstock, (TL) ©PMichael Photoz/AKA/PhotoLibrary Group, Inc., (T) Kelly Delaney; **17** (T) ©Greg Vaughn/Pacific Stock, (CR, BR) ©GSFC/NASA; **18** (C) ©Michelle Lane/Alamy Images; **19** (B) ©Matthias Kulka/Corbis, (T) Jupiter Images; **30** (CR) ©Tom Merton/Getty Images; **31** (C) ©Art Wolfe/Getty Images; **32** (R) ©Royalty-Free/Corbis, (T) Getty Images, (C) ©Philip Marazz/Corbis; **33** (B) ©Royalty-Free/Corbis, (T) Fuse/Getty Images, (R) PhotoSpin; **34** (TR, B) Getty Images; **35** Getty Images, (T) ©Tim Davis/Getty Images; **36** (T) ©Frank Lukasseck/zefa/Corbis; **37** (CR, B) Getty Images; **38** (T) ©Royalty-Free/Corbis, (T) ©Winfried Wisniewski/zefa/Corbis; **39** (B) Fuse/Getty Images; **40** (B) ©Ron Austing/Frank Lane Picture Agency/Corbis, (TR) ©The Image Bank/Getty Images; **41** (T) ©Thomas Kitchin & Victoria Hurst/Getty Images; **42** (B) Getty Images, (T) ©Tim Davis/Corbis; **43** (B) ©SilksatSunrise Photography/Alamy; **44** (C) Melissa Farlow/Getty Images; **45** (T) Natalie Fobes/Getty Images, (R) The Image Bank/Getty Images; **46** (B) ©Royalty-Free/Corbis, (TR, TC) PhotoSpin; **47** (T) Philip Marazz/Corbis; **48** (T) ©Joshua R. Meyer; **49** (TR) ©Royalty-Free/Corbis, (T) Getty Images; **50** (TR) Getty Images, (T) ©Jack Sullivan/Alamy Images; **51** (T) ©Royalty-Free/Corbis; **52** (T) ©Catherine Karnow/Corbis; **53** (T) ©Royalty-Free/Corbis, (BR) PhotoSpin; **54** (CR, CC, B) ©Joel Rheinberger/Australian Broadcasting Corporation and ABC Online; **55** (TR, B) ©Birdhouse City; **56** (BR) Getty Images; **57** (C) ©Nick Vedros & Assoc/Getty Images, (CC, C) ©Stuart McClymont/Getty Images; **58** (BR) ©Kevin Schafer/Getty Images; **59** (T) ©Joe McDonald/Corbis, (CR) ©Blend Images/Getty Images; **60** (TR) ©Blend Images/Getty Images; **61** (BR) Stockbyte; **62** (B) ©Johnny Johnson/Getty Images, (T) Getty Images; **64** (BC) ©Brian Stablyk/Getty Images; **65** (B) ©Suzy Allman/Aurora Photos; **66** (R) Getty Images; **67** (BL) Fotosearch; **68** (CC) ©Michael DeYoung/Corbis, (C) ©Royalty-Free/Corbis; **78** (B) ©Steve Bly/Alamy, (CL) Creatas; **79** (BC) Getty Images, (CR) ©John Warden/Index Stock Imagery; **80** (B) ©Alaska Stock LLC/Alamy, (T) Getty Images; **81** (TR) ©Joe McDonald/Corbis, (B) Getty Images; **82** (BR) ©The Image Bank/Getty Images; **83** (C) Getty Images; **84** (C) ©Neo Vision/Getty Images; **85** (T) ©Bob Elsdale/Getty Images, (BL) Getty Images, (BL) Mike Dunning/©DK Images; **86** (L) ©Bob Elsdale/Getty Images, (C) ©John Lund/Getty Images; **87** (TL) ©Kennan Ward/Corbis, (L) Getty Images, (T) ©Warren Bolster/Getty Images; **89** (C) ©Philip A. McDaniel/Corbis; **90** (R) ©Stockbyte, (T) ©Pete Turner/Getty Images; **91** (B) ©ARKO DATTA/Reuters/Corbis; **92** (B) Roy Toft/Getty Images; **93** (T) ©Benjamin Lowy/Corbis, (BR) ©Joel Sartore/Getty Images; **94** (T) ©Arthur Morris/Corbis, (BR) ©Neo Vision/Getty Images; **95** (BR) ©Michael Newman/PhotoEdit; **104** (C) ©Image Source/Getty Images; **105** (B) Mike Dunning/©DK Images; **106** (BL) Mike Dunning/©DK Images; **107** (TR, B) Mike Dunning/©DK Images; **108** (TR, BR) Getty Images; **109** ©Tom Stewart/Corbis; **110** (CR) Getty Images; **111** (CL) Stefano Paltera/©American Solar Challenge; **112** ©Image Source/Getty Images; **114** (C) ©ITTC Productions/Getty Images; **115** ©ITTC Productions/Getty Images; **116** ©Stone/Getty Images; **117** Getty Images; **118** ©Reuters/Corbis; **119** Getty Images; **120** (B) Getty Images, (TL) ©Yoshiko Kusano/AP/Wide World Photos; **122** Getty Images; **123** ©Laureen Middley/Getty Images; **124** (B) Stefano Paltera/©American Solar Challenge; **125** (TC) Stefano Paltera/©American Solar Challenge; **126** (B) Stefano Paltera/©American Solar Challenge; **127** (TCR) Stefano Paltera/©American Solar Challenge; **128** (T) Stefano Paltera/©American Solar Challenge; **129** (B) Stefano Paltera/©American Solar Challenge; **130** (TL, TCR, BC) Stefano Paltera/©American Solar Challenge; **131** (CR, B) Stefano Paltera/©American Solar Challenge; **132** (BR, BL) Courtesy of Air & Waste Management Association, (TR, C) Getty Images; **133** (BR, BL) Courtesy of Air & Waste Management Association; **134** (CR) Stefano Paltera/©American Solar Challenge; **136** (B) Getty Images; **137** (CR) Digital Vision; **138** (T) Getty Images; **139** (CR) ©John Warden/Index Stock Imagery; **140** (B) ©FogStock/Index Open; **141** (TR) Digital Vision; **142** (CR) Getty Images; **143** (C) Getty Images.